RACIAL JUSTICE IN AMERICA
INDIGENOUS PEOPLES
INDIAN REMOVAL

T0026762

HEATHER BRUEGL

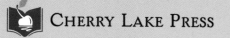

Published in the United States of America by Cherry Lake Publishing Group
Ann Arbor, Michigan
www.cherrylakepublishing.com

Reading Adviser: Beth Walker Gambro, MS, Ed., Reading Consultant, Yorkville, IL
Cover Art: Felicia Macheske

Produced by Focus Strategic Communications Inc.

Photo Credits: © OJUP/Shutterstock, 5; National Portrait Gallery, Smithsonian Institution; gift of Betty A. and Lloyd G. Schermer, 9; National Museum of the American Indian, Smithsonian Institute, 11; © Sunshower Shots/Shutterstock, 13; U.S. National Park Service, 15; JFLO217, Public domain via Wikimedia Commons, 21; Brent Moore via Flickr, CC BY-NC 2.0 DEED, 22, 23; Library of Congress, 25; William S. Prettyman, Public domain via Wikimedia Commons, 27; Smithsonian Virtual Archives, 29; © Helena GARCIA HUERTAS/Shutterstock, 30

Library of Congress Cataloging-in-Publication Data

Names: Bruegl, Heather, author.
Title: Indian removal / by Heather Bruegl.
Description: Ann Arbor, Michigan : Cherry Lake Publishing, [2024]. | Series: Racial justice in America: Indigenous peoples | Audience: Grades 7-9 | Summary: "The Trail of Tears stands as a hallmark of the pain and displacement Indigenous peoples endured, but it was not the whole story. Readers will be introduced to the many removals that occurred throughout the United States and how those acts shaped Indigenous cultures today. The Racial Justice in America: Indigenous Peoples series explores the issues specific to the Indigenous communities in the United States in a comprehensive, honest, and age-appropriate way. This series was written by Indigenous historian and public scholar Heather Bruegl, a citizen of the Oneida Nation of Wisconsin and a first-line descendant Stockbridge Munsee. The series was developed to reach children of all races and encourage them to approach race, diversity, and inclusion with open eyes and minds"— Provided by publisher.
Identifiers: LCCN 2023043590 | ISBN 9781668937945 (hardcover) | ISBN 9781668938980 (paperback) | ISBN 9781668940327 (ebook) | ISBN 9781668941676 (pdf)
Subjects: LCSH: Indian Removal, 1813-1903—Juvenile literature. | Indians, Treatment of—United States—Juvenile literature.
Classification: LCC E98.R4 B78 2024 | DDC 323.1197—dc23/eng/20231012
LC record available at https://lccn.loc.gov/2023043590

Cherry Lake Publishing would like to acknowledge the work of the Partnership for 21st Century Learning, a network of Battelle for Kids. Please visit Battelle for Kids online for more information.

Printed in the United States of America

Note from publisher: Websites change regularly, and their future contents are outside of our control. Supervise children when conducting any recommended online searches for extended learning opportunities.

Heather Bruegl, Oneida Nation of Wisconsin/Stockbridge-Munsee is a Madonna University graduate with a Master of Arts in U.S. History. Heather is a public historian and decolonial educator and travels frequently to present on Indigenous history, including policy and activism. In the Munsee language, Heather's name is Kiishookunkwe, meaning sunflower in full bloom.

CHAPTER 1

What Was Indian Removal?

Indigenous peoples were the first to live on the land that is now the United States. Some Indigenous cities had as many people as the largest cities in Europe at the time. Indigenous peoples had their own forms of government and their own trade systems. They flourished without interference. Indigenous roads connected villages and nations. Many roads we still use today began as Indigenous routes. Indigenous peoples also sailed on rivers, lakes, and along coasts.

Indigenous peoples managed the land they lived on. They cared for forests and planted crops. Their farmland stretched across field after field. They built canals to water crops in dry climates. They tapped maple trees in the North and made syrup. Indigenous peoples knew their homelands.

Wahunsenacawh, known as Powhatan, led as many as 20,000 people when the British first arrived on their land.

When Europeans first began making regular trips to North America, life began to change. Europeans started establishing trade networks with Indigenous peoples. Wealth and power began to shift relationships between different eastern Indigenous groups. European settlers eventually began to build permanent colonies. Colonizing Europeans forced Indigenous peoples off their lands. This removal became a way of life.

With every new European colony, Indigenous peoples lost more and more land. Wars and conflicts between the European settlers and Indigenous groups became common. Indigenous peoples put up strong resistance. They formed alliances with the European nation who they believed would best serve their interest. Initially, many sided with the French over the British. Then, many sided with the British over the Americans. The British made promises to leave Indigenous lands alone. The newly formed United States of America continued to grow westward.

Treaties were often used to remove Indigenous peoples from their land. U.S. government agents made promises to Indigenous leaders. Those promises were often broken. White settlers continued to move onto

Indigenous land. They took over Indigenous farms and orchards. The U.S. government sent forces to protect the settlers. The land was taken by force.

In the 19th century, settlers were moving into Alabama and Mississippi. These settlers asked the government to remove Indigenous peoples already living there.

One of the first major conflicts between British settlers and Indigenous peoples was the Pequot War (1636-1637). The Pequot Nation lived alongside British settlers. The settlers kept moving farther onto Pequot land. The Pequot people eventually promised all trade to the Dutch. This angered the British colonists.

English settlers from the Massachusetts Bay, Connecticut, and Saybrook colonies joined forces with Narragansett and Mohegan peoples. Together, they attacked the Pequot. The Pequot nearly defeated them. In response, the British-led forces burned Pequot homes. Hundreds of Pequot men, women, and children were killed. The Pequot eventually abandoned their homeland and scattered. Many were killed or enslaved. The English claimed all the Pequot land for themselves.

Both Presidents Jefferson and Monroe had proposed that Indigenous peoples could trade their lands in the East for lands in the West. This was never enforced or followed through with.

During the War of 1812, a group of Creek people sided with Great Britain. In 1814, Major General Andrew Jackson defeated the Creeks at the Battle of Horseshoe Bend. Jackson forced a treaty on the Creeks. They had to surrender over 20 million acres (8 million hectares) of their land. Today, this land makes up half of the state of Alabama and a fifth of the state of Georgia.

This was the beginning of an official policy of Indigenous removal. Jackson created 9 of the 11 significant treaties designed to force Indigenous peoples off their lands. Jackson didn't think there was room in the United States for Indigenous peoples. He believed they needed to be forced out. Then, America would be stronger.

Menawa led the Creek against Jackson in the Battle of Horseshoe Bend.
He survived and was eventually forced to relocate West in his seventies.

CHAPTER 2

The Indian Removal Act

Andrew Jackson became president of the United States in 1829. There were only 24 states in the Union at this time. Jackson, along with many White politicians, wanted Indigenous people out of the United States.

On May 28, 1830, Jackson signed the Indian Removal Act, which became law. This act allowed the president to give unsettled land west of the Mississippi River to Indigenous peoples. In exchange, the Indigenous people would give up their lands within existing state borders.

The U.S. government named this area west of the Mississippi Indian Territory. Today, that territory is the state of Oklahoma and parts of Kansas.

This map shows some of the nations Jackson and other leaders hoped to remove from existing state borders.

The Choctaws were the first Indigenous people to sign a removal treaty and begin moving west, though some refused to leave and stayed behind. This same refusal was occurring in many Indigenous groups. A small group of Seminoles were forced to sign a removal treaty. Many Seminoles refused to leave. This led to the Second Seminole War.

This statue in Florida shows Abiaka leading women and children to safety.

The Seminole Wars

The Seminoles are an Indigenous people that banded together because of removal. Conflict with settlers forced Creek and other Indigenous peoples to flee their home. They fled to Florida, which had been claimed by Spain. These **displaced** people built a community and joined with other Indigenous peoples. Together, they formed a new Indigenous group and called themselves Seminole.

In 1817, Andrew Jackson invaded Spanish Florida and attacked the Seminole. Spain agreed to give control of Florida to the United States.

In 1835, the U.S. government tried to force the Seminole to leave Florida, but they fought back. Abiaka, also known as Sam Jones, led the Seminole deep into the Everglades. The Second Seminole War was very expensive for the United States. It lasted until 1842. Most Seminoles were forced to surrender and moved to Oklahoma. Some remained and are still in Florida today. They are the unconquered.

The Creeks refused to leave, too. They signed a treaty that would guarantee them protection rights over their land. The treaty did not protect them from settlers, though. In 1836, the Creeks were forcibly removed from their homelands.

The Chickasaws decided it was safer not to resist removal. They signed a treaty with the federal government for land in the West. The treaty also protected them until they moved. However, White settlers threatened the Chickasaws. The federal government did not want to fight its own people, so it backed out of the treaty. The Chickasaws moved west. Without the treaty, however, the Chickasaws had no land in the West. As a result, they were forced to pay the Choctaws for the right to live on part of their land.

Indian removal happened in the North as well. The Northwest Territory included what is now Ohio, Michigan, Indiana, Illinois, Wisconsin, and parts of Minnesota. Indigenous groups in this area were smaller.

This statue memorializes the Chickasaws' arrival in their new territory.

The removal process happened a little at a time. Many Indigenous peoples had already been pushed back by European settlers. Some Shawnee, Ottawa, Potawatomi, Sauk, and Fox signed treaties and moved to Indian Territory.

In 1832, the Sauk leader Black Hawk led a band of Sauk and Fox back to their Illinois homeland. This led to the Black Hawk War. Indigenous groups that were further east, like the Lenape and Kickapoo, were removed from Michigan, Indiana, and Ohio. They were forced into Indian Territory. Most Potawatomi were forced off their land in 1838 and resettled in Kansas. The Miami were forced to move to Indian Territory in the 1840s.

Intertribal powwows today bring Indigenous peoples together to celebrate their strengths and the resilience of their cultures.

CHAPTER 3

The Cherokee and the Trail of Tears

The Cherokee fought removal in a different way. They assimilated as much as possible. They educated their children in Western schools, learned English, and converted to Christianity. They sometimes became plantation owners and enslavers. But none of this saved the Cherokee Nation from removal.

In 1831, the Cherokee took their case to the Supreme Court. The case was called *Worchester v. Georgia*. The tribe argued they should be allowed to stay on their land. They cited a Georgia law that stated that White settlers couldn't live on Indigenous land without written permission from the state.

The Supreme Court of the United States ruled in favor of the Cherokee. It stated that the Cherokee had the right to govern themselves. The state of Georgia, however, refused to enforce the law. President Jackson refused to uphold the decision of the Supreme Court.

After winning their Supreme Court case, the Cherokee people were divided about what to do next. President Jackson pressured them to move. A few hundred Cherokee thought this was the best option. Approximately 500 Cherokee met with U.S. officials and signed a treaty. This was the Treaty of New Echota. Principal Chief John Ross protested this treaty. He asked Congress not to ratify it. He presented a petition with over 15,000 signatures.

John Ross, principal chief of the Cherokee Nation

The U.S. government ignored the petition. The U.S. Senate ratified the treaty and it became law.
The Cherokee were given 2 years to move voluntarily. By 1838, however, 16,000 Cherokee men, women, and children remained on their land.

Martin Van Buren was now president of the United States. President Van Buren sent 7,000 U.S. troops to force the Cherokee to move at gunpoint. The Cherokee were not allowed time to gather their belongings. They were forced to leave with what they had on their backs. White settlers looted Cherokee homes as they left.

Cherokee lands included large parts of Georgia, Alabama, and Tennessee. The U.S. troops forced the Cherokee people into detention camps. These camps were in Tennessee and Alabama. They were kept there throughout the summer of 1838. Lack of water caused by a drought made travel impossible. The Cherokee people grew weaker and became sick.

Finally, in October, they began the march to Oklahoma. Armed troops pushed them forward throughout the journey. Different groups traveled different routes. Some traveled north through Kentucky, Illinois, and Missouri. Others traveled south through Mississippi and Arkansas.

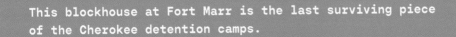

This blockhouse at Fort Marr is the last surviving piece of the Cherokee detention camps.

The Cherokee took with them 5,000 horses and 654 wagons. Many walked while carrying heavy packs. A respected Cherokee leader led each group. Each group was also accompanied by a doctor. For over 1,000 miles (1,609.34 kilometers), the Cherokee marched. They marched through blizzards and freezing winter weather. They held funerals and burials along the way. Malnutrition, disease, exhaustion, and the cold killed thousands.

The Blythe Ferry Cherokee Removal Memorial in Tennessee includes a display of seven panels listing the 2,537 heads of household forced to relocate. Many did not survive.

This forced march west became known as the Trail of Tears. Along the way, 4,000 Cherokee people died. Nearly one-fourth of the entire Cherokee population was killed. While the Trail of Tears stands out for its death toll, it was just one of many forced removals. By the 1840s, only one small band of Seminoles lived in the entire southern United States. An estimated 50,000 Indigenous people were moved off their lands.

Removal opened 25 million acres (10.11 million hectares) of land to White settlers and fueled the growth of slavery across the South. A soldier who was part of the removal effort said, "I fought through the Civil War and have seen men shot to pieces and slaughtered by thousands, but the Cherokee removal was the cruelest work I ever knew."

CHAPTER 4

The General Allotment Act and Continued Land Loss

The Indian Removal Act was not the last time Indigenous peoples were moved from their land. In 1887, the General Allotment Act was introduced. It was also called the Dawes Act. Henry Dawes served as both a congressman and a senator. While in the Senate, Dawes was the chairman of the Committee on Indian Affairs. He focused on laws that attempted to solve the "Indian Problem." He thought Indigenous people were too different from U.S. citizens and that it would be best for them if they changed. He thought they should change how they lived and give up who they were.

Dawes wanted to break Indigenous lands up. The General Allotment Act divided reservation land. Allotments, or pieces of land, were assigned to individual Indigenous families. Dawes and other

Henry Dawes's impact on Indigenous peoples is still felt today.

U.S. leaders thought that land ownership would make Indigenous people give up their so-called "Indian ways." They wanted to end the Indigenous way of life.

Before the Dawes Act, reservation land was held **communally** by all members of an Indigenous group. All registered citizens of the various Indigenous groups were eligible for an allotment. In order to receive allotments, each Indigenous person had to register with the **Bureau of Indian Affairs**. The allotted land was unsuitable for farming. It was dry and crumbled. In addition to poor land quality, many Indigenous

people couldn't or wouldn't farm. It wasn't their traditional way of life. They couldn't afford farming tools.

Although Dawes had wanted to protect Indigenous land rights, the act succeeded in doing the complete opposite. Indigenous peoples had to register to get an allotment, but not every member registered. Government leaders decided that unclaimed land no longer belonged to the Indigenous people.

In 1892, the U.S. Congress opened up 2 million acres (809.37 thousand hectares) of reservation land to

Non-Indigenous settlers lined up and raced to claim cheap Indigenous land opened up in Oklahoma in 1893.

non-Indigenous settlers. They considered this land available because the Indigenous people hadn't registered to claim it.

Lone Wolf the Second was a Kiowa chief who was living in Indian Territory. His father had also been called Lone Wolf. The Kiowa lands in that territory were created by the Medicine Lodge Treaty of 1867. The treaty required that three-fourths of all Indigenous males residing in the territory, including Kiowa, Comanche, and Apache, must agree before any territory changes could be made. When Congress tried to open the land to settlers, Lone Wolf filed a legal complaint on behalf of all three Indigenous groups. The case was called *Lone Wolf v. Hitchcock*. It was heard by the U.S. Supreme Court.

The Supreme Court ruled against Lone Wolf. It decided that Congress could get rid of reservation land without Indigenous consent. The Supreme Court also said that Congress could ignore treaties with Indigenous peoples. With that one ruling, Indigenous peoples were written into law as inferior. Congress was allowed to give Indigenous land away to non-Indigenous settlers.

The lawsuit was filed by Lone Wolf the Second, also called Mamay-Day-Te, shown here.

Indigenous National Park workers across the country make caring
for the land and its resources part of their life's work.

Ninety thousand Indigenous people were left landless. They were forced to move again.

Later in the early 20th century, under the Coolidge Administration, the act was reexamined. In 1928, the Coolidge Administration found that the Dawes Act had been used to illegally take lands from Indigenous peoples. But the damage had already been done.

Indigenous land loss and removal did not stop with these two acts alone. Throughout the 20th century, Indigenous peoples continued to lose their land, whether from policy or land developers.

Regardless of how their land was lost, it is essential to recognize that all the land that makes up the United States is Indigenous land. In recent history, there have been calls to return the land to the original stewards, the Indigenous peoples. Hopefully, one day, all who live on the land will know whose land they are on and honor both it and the ancestors.

EXTEND YOUR LEARNING

BOOKS

Benoit, Petere. *The Trail of Tears*. Children's Press, New York, 2012.

Eboch, M. M. *Native American Code Talkers*. Essential Library, Minneapolis, 2016.

Loh-Hagan, Virgina. *Stand Up, Speak Out: Indigenous Rights*. 45th Parallel Press, Ann Arbor, MI, 2022.

Schwartz, Heather E. *Forced Removal: Cause and Effects of the Trail of Tears*. Capstone Press, Mankato, MN, 2015.

Sorell, Traci. *We Are Still Here! Native American Truths Everyone Should Know*. Charlesbridge, Watertown, MA, 2021.

WEBSITES

With an adult, learn more online with these suggested searches.

"National Museum of the American Indian." Smithsonian.

"Removing Native Americans from Their Land." Library of Congress.

"Trail of Tears (U.S. History)." Britannica Kids.

"Trail of Tears (We Shall Remain)." PBS Learning Media.

GLOSSARY

assimilated (uh-SI-muh-lay-tid) to join a cultural tradition or group

Bureau of Indian Affairs (BYEER-oh UHV IN-dee-uhn uh-FAIRZ) government agency that works with federally recognized American Indian nations

canals (kuh-NALS) human-made passages to bring water to an area

communally (kuh-MYOO-nuh-lee): shared between members of the same group

displaced (dis-PLAYST) people forced away from a place, usually their rightful home

General Allotment Act (JEN-ruhl uh-LAHT-muhnt AKT) an act of Congress that divided reservations into sections and assigned pieces of the land to individual registered tribal members

Indian Removal Act (IN-dee-uhn ri-MOO-vuhl AKT) a congressional act from 1830 that gave the president power to set aside land west of the Mississippi River for Eastern tribal nations; began the reservation system and was the basis for forceful removal

Indian Territory (IN-dee-uhn TER-uh-tor-ee) former area of land in the south central United States

ratify (RA-tuh-fie) legally approve of

settlers (SET-luhrs) people who first construct permanent communities in a location

Trail of Tears (TRAYL UHV TEERS) the routes to the west of the Mississippi River that Cherokee people were forced to march along resulting in many deaths

treaties (TREE-tees) written compromises between two or more sovereign governments

INDEX